"I AM" Cares: His Eyes Are on the Sparrow

"I AM" Cares:
HIS EYES ARE ON THE SPARROW

Marlowe R. Scott

Pearly Gates Publishing, LLC, Houston, Texas

"I AM" Cares: His Eyes Are on the Sparrow

"I AM" Cares:
His Eyes Are on the Sparrow

Copyright © 2018
Marlowe R. Scott

All Rights Reserved.
No portion of this publication may be reproduced, stored in any electronic system, or transmitted in any form or by any means (electronic, mechanical, photocopy, recording, or otherwise) without written permission from the publisher. Brief quotations may be used in literary reviews.

ISBN 13: 978-1-947445-16-1
Library of Congress Control Number: 2018941570

Scripture references are taken from the King James Version of the Holy Bible and used with permission from Zondervan via Biblegateway.com. Public Domain.

For information and bulk ordering, contact:
Pearly Gates Publishing, LLC
Angela Edwards, CEO
P.O. Box 62287
Houston, TX 77205
BestSeller@PearlyGatesPublishing.com

DEDICATION

Special dedication to my husband,
Andrew Scott,
Who loves the inspiring hymn,
His Eye Is on the Sparrow.
When he hears it,
the song serves as a personal testimony for him.

ACKNOWLEDGMENTS

First and foremost, praising and thanking God and our Lord and Savior Jesus Christ for salvation and the multitude of blessings afforded me. Through the talents destined just for me, my witnessing is displayed by the books written and poetry inspired in my senior years.

Secondly, to my daughter, Angela R. Edwards, who is a constant supportive standby in my literary pursuits. As CEO, Editor, and Publisher of Pearly Gates Publishing, LLC, she has successfully published my five former books—all earning Best-Seller recognition on Amazon. To Angela: Thank you and my love for using your God-given talents for countless other authors and me.

PREFACE

This book has truly been a work in progress. I love music, and *His Eye Is on the Sparrow* is among my many favorites. I wanted to compose something special for my husband, and the desire to do so kept growing.

Inspiration for this book was given to me on October 23, 2017. My husband's favorite hymn, His Eye Is on the Sparrow, ran through my mind clearly. The hymn gives a simple message: God cares. I had shared this bit of information with my daughter, Angela. It is commonplace for inspiration for my books and poems to come to me regularly during both day and night.

That same week, confirmation came when I found among my numerous African-American books, a small gem entitled *Ethel Waters: I Touched a Sparrow* by Twila Knaack. This book was, for some reason, sitting by itself and turned over on a small hallway cabinet. Once I turned it over and saw the title, I knew the time was "now". The book was published as one of Billy Graham's Crusades series. In exploring internet searches, it was clear that Ethel Waters became well-known for singing His Eye Is on the Sparrow as well as her other songs as she traveled with Billy Graham Crusades.

Yet another confirmation occurred on Friday, November 17, 2017, while in a hotel lobby getting ready to depart National Harbor, Maryland. A single sparrow settled on the back of a bench outside and looked in the glass front directly at me. A sure sign from God again!

I was excited to learn that while birds chirp and squawk, God created in the sparrow family a species that is known as a "Song Sparrow". How fitting for this book!

Marlowe R. Scott

The following short poem speaks of the sparrow and where our souls shall rest one day.

The Little Sparrow
Marlowe Scott © 2018

God created the little sparrows
That fly among the trees.
They chirp and sing throughout the day;
I hear sweet-sounding melodies.
God values each little sparrow.
He knows when one dies;
Falling to the ground.
How much more He values us,
Even when no one else is around.
God's love is all-encompassing.
He even has numbered the hairs on our heads.
As His children, we are assured and blessed,
Until our souls soar to Heaven and into His Son
Jesus' bosom we rest.

INTRODUCTION

The title *"I AM" Cares: His Eye Is on the Sparrow* says a lot.

For those who may not know or understand, "I AM" refers to God, our Heavenly Father. Throughout the Holy Bible are countless instances and testimonies attesting to "I AM" caring for humanity.

For those who have read and studied the Holy Bible for some time, you know the words "I AM" are often used in reference to God the Father speaking as well as the Son, Jesus Christ. Preachers of the Gospel have taught and expounded in countless ways the attributes of both God the Father and Jesus Christ the Son. This list is not exhaustive, but many of those qualities are shared here:

CREATOR

- World
- Seas
- Vegetation
- Animals
- Mankind

ALWAYS PRESENT

- Protects His Own

LOVES

- Provides Needs

ALL-KNOWING

- Leads the Way

PROMISE-KEEPER

- Inspires
- Communicates

HEALER

- ❖ All Infirmities

TEACHER

- ❖ Truths
- ❖ Commandments

This book is an inspiration from God in answering my desire to write and dedicate a book to my husband, Andrew Scott. The date of that occurrence is stated in the Preface with other confirmations.

When singing and/or reading the words to *His Eye Is on the Sparrow*, I pray your spirit will be encouraged.

As with my other writings, there are inspired poems throughout this story. May you enjoy them and receive their messages.

Marlowe R. Scott

My heart and soul's desire is that you truly know as you read *"I Am" Cares: His Eye Is on the Sparrow"* that "**I AM" CARES!**

"I AM" Cares: His Eyes Are on the Sparrow

THEME SCRIPTURE

The theme scripture for this truth is
Matthew 10:29-31:

*"Are not two sparrows sold for a farthing?
And one of them shall not fall
on the ground with your Father.
But the very hairs of your head are all numbered.
Fear ye not, therefore,
ye are of more value than many sparrows."*

With reference to birds, God created their wings and feathers to have definite purposes:

- ❖ Control flight
- ❖ Insulate eggs and young
- ❖ Plucked to line nests
- ❖ Expand to protect and cover young
- ❖ Colors brighter for males
- ❖ Tail feathers expand and contract
- ❖ Insulate and warm birds
- ❖ Water repellant
- ❖ Feathers have many layers
- ❖ Soft and downy on belly

As Christians, we, too, have inborn qualities to carry us through our journeys as we learn to trust and believe in God.

"I AM" Cares: His Eyes Are on the Sparrow

TABLE OF CONTENTS

DEDICATION	vi
ACKNOWLEDGMENTS	vii
PREFACE	viii
INTRODUCTION	xi
THEME SCRIPTURE	xv
ETHEL WATERS: A SONG BIRD	1
ABOUT THE HYMN	4
WINGS	8
FEAR NOT! "I AM" CARES!	12
MAN'S SUGGESTED WAYS TO CONQUER FEAR	17
HOW CHRISTIANS MAY USE THEIR FAITH TO COMBAT FEAR	18
DISCERNMENT IS NECESSARY	26
PRAYER CHANGES THINGS	32
CONCLUSION	38
AMAZON BEST-SELLING BOOKS BY MARLOWE R. SCOTT	39
INSPIRATIONAL POEMS BY MARLOWE R. SCOTT	44
ABOUT THE AUTHOR	46
APPENDIX	49

Marlowe R. Scott

"I AM" Cares: His Eyes Are on the Sparrow

ETHEL WATERS: A SONG BIRD

Have you ever heard a song that resonates and touches deeply, sometimes to tears or smile? *His Eye Is on the Sparrow* is such a hymn. Many renditions have been sung by choirs and soloists over the years. Ethel Waters was such a soloist who sang the hymn often for large and small audiences and religious services.

Following are brief notes about Ethel Waters, and also Civilla D. Martin (Knaack, 1978), who was inspired to write *His Eye Is on the Sparrow*:

1. The introduction to *Ethel Waters: I Touched a Sparrow* was written by Ruth Bell Graham, Billy Graham's wife. She stated that getting to know Ethel Waters "was one of the most enriching, merriest, most educational experiences in my life." On one occasion where she referred to Ethel as a "sparrow", Ethel asked if she could be allowed to sing in the choir at the first Madison

Square Garden meeting. This is important because Ethel Waters found salvation through a Billy Graham Crusade. Once she sang and they heard her God-blessed voice, Ethel was invited to join in many Crusade travels and sang with the choir. She became a featured soloist.

2. At that point, Ethel had no family and looked on the Graham team as her family. One of the team members was the author of the book, Twila Knaack, who came to know Ethel well. Twila worked as secretary to Billy Graham's press representative. One day, after knowing Ethel for some time, it was suggested that she write some of the experiences of the trials and happy adventures she had with Ethel, as she was probably the closest person to her as she listened to the stories Ethel shared.

3. At the funeral of Ethel Waters, a tape was played of her singing *His Eye Is on the Sparrow*. She was well-known for her part as Petunia in the well-known film "Cabin in the Sky". She sent a message by telegram to Vincente Minnelli, director of the film, as her health was failing. The message stated in part: "I want to personally invite you and each in attendance to visit me in my "Cabin in the Sky." She was known to use that invitation to everyone she met.

For anyone looking towards the promises of Heaven as our eternal home, what a great invitation — one I believe touched and changed many!

ABOUT THE HYMN

His Eye Is on the Sparrow was written by Civilla D. Martin and published in 1905. The composer of this well-known hymn was Charles H. Gabriel. The inspiration for the hymn is based on the following three passages of scripture:

❖ Psalm 32:8 – *"I will instruct thee in the way which thou shall go: I will guide thee with mine eye."*

❖ Matthew 6:26 – *"Behold the fowls of the air; for they sow not, neither do they reap nor gather into barns; yet your Heavenly Father feedeth them. Are ye not much better than they?"*

❖ Matthew 10:29-31 – *"Are not two sparrows sold for a farthing? And one of them shall not fall on the ground with your Father. But the very hairs of your heard are all numbered. Fear ye not, therefore, ye are of more value than many sparrows."*

"I AM" Cares: His Eyes Are on the Sparrow

Like so many hymn writers, Civilla Martin was inspired to write *His Eye Is on the Sparrow* after an incident that happened. She and her husband were visiting friends in Elmira, New York who were both ill but were happy. When asked how they remained so bright and hopeful, Mrs. Doolittle replied, "His eye is on the sparrow, and I know He watches me!" Those words ignited the imagination of Mrs. Martin, and the song was written!

His Eye Is on the Sparrow **Hymn**

VERSE 1:
Why should I feel discouraged?
Why should the shadows come?
Why should my heart be lonely,
And long for Heav'n and home?
When Jesus is my portion;
My constant Friend is He.
His eye is on the sparrow,
And I know He watches me;
His eye is on the sparrow,
And I know He watches me.

REFRAIN:
I sing because I'm happy.
I sing because I'm free.
For His eye is on the sparrow,
And I know He watches me.

"I AM" Cares: His Eyes Are on the Sparrow

VERSE 2:
"Let not your heart be troubled";
His tender word I hear,
And resting on His goodness,
I lose my doubts and fears;
Though by the path He leadeth,
But one step I may see.
His eye is on the sparrow,
And I know He watches me.
His eye is on the sparrow,
And I know He watches me.

VERSE 3:
Whenever I am tempted,
Whenever clouds arise,
When songs give place to sighing,
When hope within me dies;
I draw the closer to Him,
From care, He sets me free.
His eye is on the sparrow,
And I know He watches me.
His eye is on the sparrow,
And I know He watches me.

Marlowe R. Scott

WINGS (Brent, 1947)
~ A Poem ~

The poem "Wings" was discovered in my mother's favorite book of poetry titled *Alabaster Boxes*. She read many poems from it over the years, and I treasure it.

I invite you to enjoy and share it with others as encouragement.

"I AM" Cares: His Eyes Are on the Sparrow

Three little birds lay in a nest,
All cozy and safe and warm,
And the mother bird was hovering near,
To shield them from danger and harm.
She brought them worms of the choicest kind,
She fed them from day to day;
And her love, like a great warm blanket,
Sheltered them where they lay.

But her babies were restless and ill at ease,
And filled with a strange alarm,
And the mother grieved that they fretted so,
Knowing them safe from harm.
And she said, "What ails you, my children dear?
Why do you grumble and squirm?
Be good, and mother will fly away
And bring you a nice fat worm."

But they teased and worried her all the more
And showed her their little wings;
And they said, "It is these that fret us so,
These naked, ugly things.
They hang by our sides and weight us down,
They worry us day by day.
Is there no way to get rid of them?
What use are they anyway?"

And the mother said, "O you foolish birds.
You are naughty to grumble so;
They are nice little wings and may prove some day
A blessing for all you know."
So, the days went by with their sun and shade,
And the birdies kept free from harm,
And then one day there passed their way
A terrible, fierce windstorm.

It blew the birds from their sheltered nest,
And they screamed aloud with fright
As they felt themselves hurled here and there
With the wind's terrific might;
Then, all of a sudden, they knew not how,
The weights that hung at their side
Became in a moment stanch little wings
That bore them above the tide.

Up from the wild storm's lash and roar,
Happy and glad and free,
Each naughty birdie found itself
In the top of the highest tree.
And I sometimes think we are like those birds,
Grumbling and raising sand
About the fetters that weight us down,
That we cannot understand.

"I AM" Cares: His Eyes Are on the Sparrow

Now, the dear Lord knew when He made those birds,
Along with a voice to sing,
They would need to travel the paths of air,
On each side a stout little wing
And He never has made a creature yet,
A nation or race or creed,
And nailed or pinned to it anywhere
A thing that it did not need.

And He knows the way that His children take,
And He watches wherever we go,
And He'll send His love as a beacon light,
To brighten each path of woe.
O my dears, the troubles that press till
Our souls almost touch the sod
May prove someday to be beautiful wings
That will bear us away to God.

FEAR NOT! "I AM" CARES!

I have heard over the last few years and most recently sermons, teachings, inspired words of pastors and other Christians about fear. This peaked my interests, as I have read many scriptures, books, and social media posts on the subject.

His Eye Is on the Sparrow speaks of times when we may feel discouraged, lonely, and even unsure of our future. A sense of fear can occur, and we must pray and find ways to overcome and hold out until peace returns.

Prayerfully, the sharing of the following will provide comfort during those times.

You may have read, and personally, I have heard about fear and trembling times before God. This was in the fire-and-brimstone form of preaching when I was a child. Because of that, I was afraid of God but loved Jesus. My young mind did not fully understand that they are one in the same — The Trinity.

Scripture reference is found in Exodus 14:31 and illustrates how Israel felt after God destroyed the Egyptians:

"And Israel saw that great work which the LORD did upon the Egyptians: and the people feared the LORD, and believed the LORD, and His servant Moses."

This refers to the miracles and other occurrences that God performed in Israel's presence: the plagues, death angel killing firstborn (to include Pharaoh's son), and parting the sea so Israel could cross safely and then the sea closed the path and Pharaoh's army perished in the waters.

- ❖ Psalm 2:11 – *"Serve the LORD with fear, and rejoice with trembling."*

- ❖ Proverbs 9:10 – *"The fear of the LORD is the beginning of wisdom: and the knowledge of the Holy is understanding."*

These scriptures may seem to contradict protection by God or are misunderstood. In the above verses, fear is better defined as being worshipful toward God and having reverential respect.

Proverbs 9:10 clearly associates wisdom, knowledge of what is holy, and understanding as the ways to begin showing reverence to God and, likewise, Jesus as Christians.

In Luke 1:12, it is recorded what Zacharias saw and felt afraid when an angel appeared to him and foretold the birth of John the Baptist:

- ❖ *"And when Zacharias saw him, he was troubled, and fear fell upon him."*

That verse showed how fear gripped one of God's servant, yet he became blessed as father of John the Baptist!

Although I am not personally able to comprehend the increased feeling of fear, especially in the Christian's life, it became clear that it is real to those who have not read, believed, and applied God's Word to their spiritual life. As we may know, the Christian's approach in handling times of fear are not as the world (unsaved) react when those times come. As humans, we are afraid for many reasons. Some have learned fear from bad experiences, such as a dog bite while young. As one grows older, that experience makes them afraid of dogs. How about times you have viewed people being killed by snake venom or being squeezed to death by a Boa Constrictor? Yes—*Fear, Fear, Fear!*

The "fear list" is endless and growing, to include fear of:

- ❖ Heights
- ❖ Thunder/Lightning
- ❖ Small spaces
- ❖ Crowds
- ❖ Insects (spiders, wasps, bees, etc.)
- ❖ Speaking in public
- ❖ DYING
- ❖ Dogs
- ❖ Birds

Medical professionals, books, therapists, and many human methods are used to calm our fears. A few suggestions follow and may be helpful.

MAN'S SUGGESTED WAYS TO CONQUER FEAR
(Some of these methods also help Christians.)

- ❖ Take time out / Go for nature walk
- ❖ Breathe through panic
- ❖ Examine the evidence / Read
- ❖ Visualize a happy place
- ❖ Talk about it / Get support
- ❖ Promote positive versus negative results
- ❖ Find root of the fear
    - o Taught from parents, friends, or school (dark, unlit places/alleys, open wells, sewers)
    - o Learned from experiences (fire burns; walking on and falling through dangerous ice)
- ❖ Journaling / Getting them out of your mind
- ❖ Exercising releases stress/fear

HOW CHRISTIANS MAY USE THEIR FAITH TO COMBAT FEAR

The acronym below is familiar to many, both in and out of work, training sessions, and publications. Churches also have incorporated this factual-based material for years. I also found other interpretations on websites and social media. **FEAR** is said to be:

> **F**alse
>
> **E**vidence
>
> **A**ppearing
>
> **R**eal

At the suggestion from my daughter, I also found words of my own to fit **FEAR** which have applied to me:

> **F**aith
>
> **E**mbraced
>
> **A**ttacks
>
> **R**elinquished

This brief explanation is offered. Appropriate scriptures may be helpful in understanding.

F – Faith: Those who are Christians have God and Jesus Christ. Their attributes protect and bless us.

- Psalm 56:3 – *"What time I am afraid, I will trust in thee."*
- 2 Timothy 1:7 – *"For God hath not given us the spirit of fear; but of power, and of love, and of a sound mind."*
- 1 John 4:18 – *"There is no fear in love; but perfect love casteth out fear: because fear hath torment. He that feareth is not made perfect in love."*

E – Embraced: Through faith and beliefs in the biblical truths of conquered fear, situations are taken and applied to our personal situation at any particular time.

- ❖ Deuteronomy 31:6 – *"Be strong and of good courage; fear not, not be afraid of them: for the LORD thy God, He it is that doth go with thee; He will not fail thee, nor forsake thee."*
- ❖ Joshua 1:9 – *"Have I not commanded thee? Be strong and of good courage; be not afraid, neither be thou dismayed: for the LORD thy God is with thee whithersoever thou goest."*

A – Attacks: With the embraced confidence and applied spiritual strength, we are able to meet the fearful situation head-on.

- ❖ Psalm 23:4 – *"Yea, though I walk through the valley of the shadow of death, I will fear no evil: for thou art with me; thy rod and thy staff they comfort me."*
- ❖ Isaiah 41:10 – *"Fear thou not; for I am with thee: be not dismayed; for I am thy God: I will strengthen thee; yea, I will help thee; yea, I will uphold thee with the right hand of my righteousness."*

R – Relinquished: Our cares are given over to Jesus' Holy Spirit through prayers and confident actions as the Holy Spirit directs. We are delivered from the fears.

- ❖ Psalm 34:4 – *"I sought the LORD, and He heard me and delivered me from all my fears."*
- ❖ Psalm 118:6 – *"The LORD is on my side; I will not fear: What can man do unto me?"*

Why not use your ideas and inspiration to develop an acronym for **FEAR** below?

F _____

E _____

A _____

R _____

"I AM" Cares: His Eyes Are on the Sparrow

Based on the question in Psalm 118:6, I was blessed to receive the following inspired poem:

Whom Shall I Fear?
Marlowe Scott © 2018

What can man do to me?
Harm my body? Yes.
Harm my soul? NO!
I AM God's child.
Angels protect my SOUL,
And because of that,
Heaven remains my GOAL.
In Heaven, I'll see Jesus;
My Master, Savior, and King.
I will have the peace and JOY
Only Heavenly realms can bring!
Promises will be fulfilled.
I will rest and shout "HALLELUJAH!"
Jesus, the Lord, my Protector I will see.
What can man do to me?

"I AM" Cares: His Eyes Are on the Sparrow

Q: What are you afraid of and how do or did you handle it?

Q: Does Holy Scripture address or comfort you when fearful? Why or why not?

DISCERNMENT IS NECESSARY

As an effective method, I am blessed with the ability to address and better understand scriptures through discernment. This blessing to apply discernment to God's Word came after earnest prayer time with God.

My prayers were answered, as now, I have clearer meaning and application to my spiritual walk of scripture. I strongly suggest you do personal studies and pray for this wonderful Christian characteristic.

Discernment and the ability to perceive what the scriptures mean can be challenging, especially since God's ways are not the world's ways of doing things in this life.

I have shared in a prior publication how I prayed and sought God to give me the ability to truly discern and understand scriptures. My prayers were answered, and I was truly blessed!

I must add here that cross-references in the Holy Bible, Concordances, and other scripture helps are still a part of my study time. However, once my spiritual eye was able to discern what I read and, more importantly, heard from preachers, spiritual leaders, teachers, and friends, it was easier to determine what was correct or a misinterpretation.

Many preachers have clearly stated that we, as Christians, need to be able to clearly state what and why we believe in Jesus Christ and the scriptures. Or, like some of the pastors in years past said, "You got to know that you know!"

What does discernment have to do with fear? I believe that knowing what the Bible clearly states when God's people were experiencing fearful situations gives the answer.

- ❖ Proverbs 1:2 – *"To know wisdom and instruction; to perceive the words of understanding…"*
- ❖ Proverbs 2:11 – *"Discretion shall preserve thee, understanding shall keep thee…"*
- ❖ Jeremiah 5:21 – *"Hear now this, O foolish people, and without understanding; which have eyes, and see not; which have ears, and hear not…"*
- ❖ Luke 12:56 – *"Ye hypocrites, ye can discern the face of the sky and of the earth; but how is it that ye do not discern this time?"*
- ❖ Hebrews 5:14 – *"But strong meat belongeth to them that are of full age, even those who by reason of use have their senses exercised to discern both good and evil."*
- ❖ 2 Timothy 3:7 – *"Ever learning and never able to come to the knowledge of the truth."*

"I AM" Cares: His Eyes Are on the Sparrow

Q: How do those six scriptures speak to you?

Q: What ways have you used to gain a clearer understanding of scripture?

Q: Have you prayed and sought after discernment, growth, using spiritual gifts, or other Christian qualities and received the answer? If not, what are you doing or plan on doing to receive your need/growth in that area?

_____
_____
_____
_____
_____
_____
_____
_____
_____
_____
_____
_____
_____
_____
_____
_____
_____
_____

PRAYER CHANGES THINGS

There are many helpful resources on how to develop an effective prayer life. One is an excellent Holy Bible resource FREE on the internet: YouVersion app. It can be found at www.bible.com. It contains inspirations for the day, devotionals, and is available for in-depth studies. There are 1,000+ versions and languages.

God knows what we need of before we ask. You may be familiar with **P.U.S.H.** (Pray Until Something Happens). While this is true, I found at times, simple, short prayers get answered, too!

In my first book, *Spiritual Growth: From Milk to Strong Meat*, I shared how just saying "JESUS!" stopped a vehicle from rear-ending my car on the way home from work.

Another more recent incident occurred when a simple prayer of less than seven words was answered when my home phone was partially disabled after a severe winter storm. One Sunday morning, after almost two weeks of not being able to call out or retrieve messages, I looked at the unit it was connected to and turned the switch off and then back on after asking God to help me. IMMEDIATELY, everything began working again! Needless to say, I told family and friends about THAT blessing!

There are many more instances, and I am sure someone reading this has had similar and more dramatic prayer-answering testimonies. My purpose is to share that God cares about EVERYthing His children go through! Remember: Nothing is too hard or minute for Him to handle.

Take time to jot down your personal instances of where you know God has worked or is still working something out for you.

"I AM" Cares: His Eyes Are on the Sparrow

Share and make notes here of ways God has answered your prayers. Have you testified to others about those answers?

_____
_____
_____
_____
_____
_____
_____
_____
_____
_____
_____
_____
_____
_____
_____
_____
_____
_____
_____
_____
_____

Before concluding, I offer these poems for your spiritual edification. May you feel blessed as I was blessed to compose them with God's inspiration.

God Cares
Marlowe Scott © 2018

If God watches and cares for a sparrow,
I know He surely cares for me.
He proved His everlasting love for us
When His Son, Jesus, died on a rugged tree.
There, Jesus bore our sins upon Himself,
Making a way for us to repent and believe in Him;
And one day have our souls fly to glory,
Then join in that HALLELUJAH CHORUS, singing:
"PRAISE GOD! PRAISE GOD!
I AM IN THE PRESENCE OF THE KING!"

I Do Not Die
Marlowe Scott © 2018

My soul and spirit live forever
In my family and lives I have touched.
I know this is true because
Jesus has changed me and loves me very much!
When I breathe my last,
I am assured that I will be blessed
To be in Heaven with Jesus
As my eternal reward.

CONCLUSION

"I AM's" love and protection for us cannot be equaled and fully appreciated as well as embraced by human standards. He loves the smallest element of our lives—each hair, pain, and tear—I AM knows and numbers our days on this earth.

To understand all of this, we must be born again through admitting our sins, asking God for forgiveness, believing in Jesus Christ, and becoming Christians. We need unwavering faith, an effective prayer life, and study the Holy Bible's scriptures along with learning how to apply them to our life.

As "I AM" clearly cares for the sparrow, I know…and you can know with all certainty that He cares for us. You are invited to experience His love today!

"I AM" Cares: His Eyes Are on the Sparrow

Amazon Best-Selling Books Written by Marlowe R. Scott

Spiritual Growth: From Milk to Strong Meat
© 2015

AMAZON BEST-SELLER
Available for purchase at:
http://bit.ly/MilkToMeat

Marlowe R. Scott

Believing Without Seeing: The Power of Faith
© 2015

AMAZON BEST-SELLER
Available for purchase at:
http://bit.ly/BelievingWithoutSeeing

"I AM" Cares: His Eyes Are on the Sparrow

Keeping It Real: The Straight and Narrow
© 2016

AMAZON BEST-SELLER
Available for purchase at
http://bit.ly/KIRPbk

Marlowe R. Scott

Worth the Journey: The Train Ride to Glory
(3 Books in 1)
© 2016

AMAZON #1 BEST-SELLER
Available for purchase in paperback at:
http://bit.ly/WorthTheJourneyPaperback

Available for purchase in hardcover at:
http://bit.ly/WorthTheJourneyHardback

"I AM" Cares: His Eyes Are on the Sparrow

Never Alone: Intimate Times with Jesus
© 2017

AMAZON #1 BEST-SELLER
Available for purchase at:
http://bit.ly/NeverAlonePbk

Marlowe R. Scott

INSPIRATIONAL POEMS BY MARLOWE R. SCOTT

Jesus, My Friend Jesus

Kinship Benefits

Songs in the Night

Higher Spiritual Heights

The Sheepfold

Growing in Faith

Abuse is Not Love

Calvary's Cross

The Announcement

The Little Sparrow

Whom Shall I Fear?

God Cares

I Do Not Die

"I AM" Cares: His Eyes Are on the Sparrow

Marlowe R. Scott
Owner/Creator

Phone: (609) 248-0051
Email: M.R.Boyce4491@gmail.com
Browns Mills, NJ

"Specializing in Hand-Crafted Creations Giving Special Comfort and LOVE"

- ❖ Memory Pillows
- ❖ Memory Quilts
- ❖ Crib Quilts
- ❖ Throws
- ❖ And much, much more!

About the Author

Marlowe R. Scott was born at home in a small, South Jersey community of Cedarville, New Jersey. Her parents were Carl and Helena Harris. Marlowe is a true country girl who loves nature—God's wondrous creation. She enjoys seeing birds preparing nests, wild turkeys roaming the backyard with their young, and the stately deer in the field and property tree line where she lives in Browns Mills, New Jersey.

Marlowe has been blessed with many talents. They include writing, poetry, music, sewing, crocheting, quilting, and floral designs. Her educational focus was the Communication Arts Degree Program at Burlington County College, as well as attendance and participation in numerous government-sponsored training venues.

Marlowe's extensive experiences encompassed duties as Leadership, Education, and Development Facilitator; Equal Employment Opportunity Counselor; Quality Management Facilitator; and member of the New Jersey Quality Board of Examiners. With her commitment to quality, she also participated in video conferences, workshops, and community volunteer activities.

One highlight of her career was a conference held in Baltimore, Maryland where she was a member of a select group of individuals who met and interacted with Retired U.S. Army General and Former U.S. Secretary of State, Colin Powell. Marlowe retired after 33 years of dedicated federal civil service.

She has taught Floral Arts and Crafts in adult education, won ribbons for her creative designs, and appeared on television. Currently, she devotes most of her time to quilting and developing her home-based business, M.R.S. Inspirations, with the motto *"Magnificent Revelations Are My Specialty"*. Her creations are focused on making special memories in lap quilts, throws, baby quilts, and pillows which show love and give comfort to the recipient.

Readers of her books have verbally expressed, as well as given written endorsements and testimonies, sharing how they were inspired, experienced spiritual growth, and comfort through her writing and poems. She also received commendation from former U.S. President Barack Obama and family for sharing with them *Spiritual Growth: From Milk to Strong Meat*.

Marlowe is married to Andrew Scott and has three children: Carl, James, and Angela, as well as five grandchildren and a host of great-grandchildren. She is currently a member of Tabernacle Baptist Church, Burlington, New Jersey.

APPENDIX

Brent, B. (1947). *Wings; Alabaster Boxes*. Win, Review and Herald Publishing Association, Takoma Park, Washington, DC.

Knaack, T. (1978). *Ethel Waters: I Touched a Sparrow; Special Crusade Edition*. Billy Graham Evangelistic Association. World Wide Publications, Minneapolis, MN.

Marlowe R. Scott

www.ingramcontent.com/pod-product-compliance
Lightning Source LLC
Chambersburg PA
CBHW071542080526
44588CB00011B/1762